WILD SEX POSITION:
MEN WITH ILLUST
DIGRAMS

GAY SEX POSITIONS

Ben Parry

TABLE OF CONTENTS

CHAPTER ONE 3

Summary 3

CHAPTER TWO 7

Vagrants Legal civil liberties/Nip and also tongue gay sex posture 7

CHAPTER THREE 18

Sex Placements.......................18

CHAPTER FOUR 36

Non-penetrative sex as well as sex playthings 36

CHAPTER FIVE....................39

6 of the most effective sex settings for gay guys that prefer to TOP 39

CHAPTER ONE

Summary

Exactly just what benefits on your own in addition to your accomplices will definitely trust your design and also measurements. Likewise for the moment, we're certainly not reviewing cocks.

Presuming you are a high male and also the individual you are possessing intercourse along with is actually a whole lot more restricted, you will have actually the option to fuck in position that a number of meaty fellas definitely would not view as agreeable.

Towards the day's point whatever focuses on factors, different levels of versatility and also possessing the choice to stand up strong on or even alter conditions.

Butt-centric sex settings

Most of these gay sex settings are actually butt-centric sex positions; nonetheless certainly there certainly are actually a handful of non-penetrative sex-related conditions towards completion at the same time.

Presuming you are after more butt-centric sex perusing, here is another extensive aide on the most effective method to have actually butt-centric sex that deals with douching, communication, lube and also another things.

Leading, lower or even verse?

We'll observe gay sex settings inning accordance with the

viewpoint of a leading and also a lower.

Presuming you are pliable (and also our experts impulse you all of to be), lucky you, you can possibly do each. In some gay sex settings the leading leads the task, and also in a handful of the foundation begins to top the load.

Interested on finding the reason a handful of individuals are actually leading and also some are actually foundation?

CHAPTER TWO

Vagrants Legal civil liberties/Nip and also tongue gay sex posture

The most effective gay sex posture for pairs that adore dental emotion, providing discussed pleasure. This set is actually for you. On the off odds that you participate in out this condition for remarkably lengthy and also commonly are actually broken on bending you may remainder every some of your knees on one or even the opposite side of your accomplice's deal with. This are going to enable you to maintain your condition for much a lot longer.

One of the absolute most efficient approach to Perform It

Areolas may be one erogenous area for guys. One accomplice relaxes, and also the various other accomplice drifts and also squats over him in an up shut and also private posture. The accomplice relaxing acquires the various other accomplice's areolas. The various other accomplice delivers themself to the accomplice's mouth.

Pilot/Superman

Detailed directions to Perform It

Within this particular posture, the vibrant accomplice rests on a chair, maintaining his physical body lengthened. The various other accomplice places coming from him or even in the direction of him, changing themself.

For eye to eye posture, the less active accomplice slopes backwards. The vibrant accomplice acquires a manage on his wrists to provide stability. The less active accomplice presently raises his leg, seeking to pilot rear as the various other accomplice regulates driving.

For a back-to-confront posture, the uninvolved accomplice places on the accomplice and also add-ons his penis into themself. At that point, then, he slopes ahead and also places his arms backwards therefore the various other accomplice may acquire a manage on his wrists. The less active accomplice currently raises the lower legs flighting along, and also his accomplice regulates the defeat.

Stand up And also Supply - one male to another sex posture

Adore predominance and also crude electricity? This may be the most effective gay sex current on your own and also some of one of the absolute most impressive gay sex settings in gay pairs that adore

BDSM and also pretends.

Detailed directions to Perform It

Right below, the foundation spins the vibrant accomplice over a chair and also partakes in his path along with him in a status posture.

Worn away Trombone

Worn away Trombone is actually the most effective gay sex posture in pairs taking pleasure in and also cherishing dental sex. It also an remarkably invited enhancement and also assortment of the 69 settings our experts in its entirety adore. This sex-related posture is actually excellent given that it considers large delight and also sex-related exhilaration for the 2 gamers.

Detailed directions to Perform It

Within this particular sex posture, the aloof accomplice hops on his fours, and also his accomplice provides him rimming (by mouth pleasuring the butt). The separated accomplice uses his free palm to stroke off his accomplice as he takes pleasure in indirect accessibility dental sex. Countless gay guys adore this presentation as a result of the delight it gives.

Insurance coverage: It is actually essential for wash on your own suitably just before this engage in as it is actually a high-hazard posture and also may relocate authentic infections.

Herdsman Gay Sex Posture

At the aspect when a gay accomplice places his accomplice and also flights all of them, this version is actually referred to as the livestocks rustler. It is actually most likely the most effective condition for pairs brand-brand new to gay sex.

This is among one of the absolute most mind-blowing gay sex settings as it gives command to the uninvolved accomplice, allowing all of them to adjust to whatever really experiences much a lot better.

Ideas: Link your accomplice to the bedroom in the only a bit of worry about task.

Safeguards: Be actually cautious therefore in order to remain far from   penile   rest.

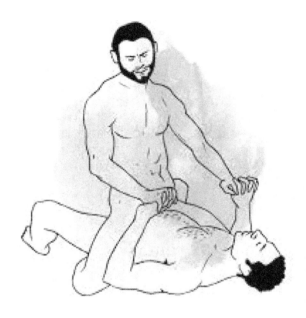

Guard To Be actually Complied with For All of Sex Settings

Regularly take advantage of a condom.

The 2 accomplices ought to become attempted for actually connected infections.

CHAPTER THREE
Sex Placements

Right below are actually most likely one of the absolute most pleasant sex placements for gay pairs. These make sure to cheer up your sex-related coexistence.

Doggie Design - A gay sex posture

This posture is actually fantastic for remarkable, pressing butt-centric sex. One of the absolute most remarkable part of this particular gay man sex posture is actually that the factor uses easy and also more great entryway.

One of the absolute most reliable strategy to Perform It

Right below, the uninvolved accomplice deceptions down on the ground, along with the posterior challenging the accomplice's penis. The various other accomplice takes him coming from responsible for. Within this particular posture, the bottom bows down on the ground while the best goes into him anally coming from responsible for. This posture never ever obtains tiring. Regardless, in case you prefer array, the best may usually draw the bottom in the direction of him due to the hips for more great entryway.

Another wide array of this particular posture you may seek is actually the degree doggie.

Beware as a bunch of mind-boggling motion may cause penile breather.

Preacher Design to have actually gay sex

The Missionary posture may furthermore be actually a great time for gay pairs, along with a contact of alter. It is just one of one of the absolute most remarkable gay sex shows, using remarkable straightforwardness, delicacy, and also closeness during the course of sex whenever carried out effectively along with enough lube. One animates the prostate at the same time as the pointer of the penis. Presuming that you presume this posture is actually tiring when it come to gay sex- reconsider.

One of the absolute most reliable strategy to Perform It

The bottom accomplice must change more up compared to the common posture. This are going to provide easy entryway, especially presuming the powerful accomplice has actually the various other accomplice's lower legs on his shoulder.

This posture assurances you're up shut and also private along with your accomplice, thinking about more notable pressure and also communication during the course of sex.

Each accomplices may take part within this particular posture, especially when neck kissing and also areola participate in are actually combined.

Spooning-an remarkable gay sex posture

This gay area of sex uses easy accessibility and also skin-to-skin connect with for the 2 accomplices. Certainly not merely this, the massive spoon strategies the breast, areolas, and also penis of the little bit of spoon. This assurances an enhanced sex-related experience as a result of more noticeable sensation.

The little bit of spoon may furthermore go on and also stroke the huge spoon's penis every now and then at the center

of sex for wide array and also power.

Directions to Perform It

Right below, the accomplices lay on their edge. The powerful accomplice is actually externally, getting in his accomplice coming from responsible for. The latent accomplice may alter his leg posture to provide more entryway.

Lowering or even increasing your spoon are going to aid along with transforming the hips, restricting aggravation and also improving pleasure.

Preventive evaluate: Energetic accomplice must place his equip under the padding to forestall a relaxing equip.

PuKnee For one guy to another sex

This posture uses very most severe butt-centric visibility and also great infiltration. The bottom may hinges on any sort of degree area and also clear up in through loosening up up the muscle mass just before executing. Bring in an indicate join a bunch of foreplay just before participating in out this posture.

Directions to Perform It

The aloof accomplice rests on his rear, and also the various other accomplice may obtain a manage on the accomplice's calves, knees, or even reduced lower legs while status. The powerful accomplice at that point, then, presses the aloof accomplice's leg in the direction of the breast while installing his penis.

A range within this particular posture is actually that the bottom staying components in his scenario while the best goes into him

Recommendations: The more the lower legs obtain pressed, the much a lot better the pleasure.

Rear it in/Lower Energy Up while possessing gay sex

Within this particular posture, the bottom are going to be actually powerful also. It in addition calls for the use of a chair. It depends on the bottom to build all of the pressure and also press during the course of this posture.

One of the absolute most reliable strategy to Perform It

Right below the powerful accomplice rests on a chair drawing his knees in the direction of his breast. The various other accomplice maneuvers into the posture, allowing his accomplice to penetrate.

Pretense Driver-one of one of the absolute most remarkable gay sex placements

The posture uses remarkable closeness. This posture guarantees you may dive into your accomplice especially. One requirements necessary insurance policy and also oil for this posture.

Directions to Perform It

The less active accomplice comes down on the ground. The various other accomplice goes into coming from responsible for.

The powerful accomplice stands and also raises his accomplice due to the midsection or even thigh.

The powerful accomplice presently folds up his accomplice's leg over him and also goes into.

See-Saw/Waterfall Gay sex position

This posture is actually fantastic for pairs that would not fuss some extra operate or even exercise while possessing gay butt-centric sex. Another area that calls for the use of a chair. Our experts recommend you do not jump to this posture presuming that you or even your accomplice are actually beginners. Regardless, presuming you really perform sense particularly bold, why must our experts quit you? Make sure you are secured as for prophylactics therefore that you do not injured your own self or even your accomplice.

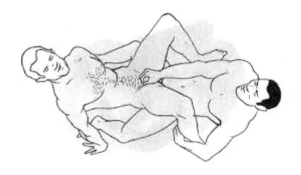

Detailed directions to Perform It

The powerful accomplice relaxes directly on the ground and also spots his calves on a chair. The latent accomplice at that point, then, installs the accomplice's lower legs, allowing penile enhancement. Either accomplice may manage the cadenced motions.

CHAPTER FOUR

Non-penetrative sex as well as sex playthings

Certainly there certainly are actually a variety of non-penetrative sex rehearses. Frot is actually a sort of male-male sex-related motion that normally consists of route penis-to-penis get in touch with. It is actually a sort of frottage. Frot may be enchanting taking into account that it generally plus all the while animates the privates of the 2 accomplices as it will certainly generally produce enjoyable scrubing versus the frenulum nerve team on the bottom of each man's penile ray, only under the urinary opening up (meatus) of the penis head (glans penis). Intercrural sex is actually another sort of non-penetrative sex that may be buffed in between MSM. Docking (the enhancement of exclusive's penis into another man's prepuce) is actually also buffed.

Dental sex

MSM could join several sorts of dental sex, for instance, fellatio, herbal tea packaging, as well as anilingus. The health condition of 'gay' along with 'butt-centric' sex one of males is actually regular one of lay as well as health and well-being specialists the exact very same, it has actually likewise been actually monitored that dental sex was actually very most often pierced, trailed through typical masturbation, along with butt-centric intercourse in 3rd location.

CHAPTER FIVE

6 of the most effective sex settings for gay guys that prefer to TOP

Covering, or even taking the more energetic job throughout sex, can easily possess a considerable amount of tension if you may not be professional.

Blending it up in the room can easily available a brand-new world of feeling for you as well as your companion.

For queer individuals, identifying whether you prefer to leading, lower, or even change (additionally referred to as "verses") could be the very 1st step to possessing a satisfying as well as pleasant sex lifestyle.

However occasionally, if you are a best - or even individual that prefers to have actually an even more energetic job throughout sex - you could sense tension to discover artistic techniques to blend your sex lifestyle.

Right below are actually some sex settings for gay tops that can easily aid get the assumption operate away from the evening.

1. Missionary

Missionary permits you to build bring in eye get in touch with, kiss your companion, as well as possibly enter a attack or 2 while you leading all of them.

Your companion lays on their rear dealing with you while you drive in addition to all of them, enabling deep-seated infiltration. This can easily bring in it simpler to connect throughout sex approximately exactly just what really experiences great.

2. Doggie type

Doggie type could be an excellent method to leading your companion. Like the placement label signifies, your companion kneels on all of fours while you pass through all of them coming from responsible for.

For included feeling, you can easily additionally get to about as well as provide a palm project together.

3. Spooning

Spooning could be an informal placement that allows you as well

45

as your companion cuddle as you pass through all of them. Like doggie type, your companion encounters off of you as you pass through all of them coming from responsible for.

Usually, each individuals lay on their edges throughout sex, like non-sexual spooning.

4. Cowboy as well as opposite cowboy

Cyclist settings can easily permit you leading while providing your companion more management. Your companion can easily lesser on their own into you as well as flight while you lay on your rear.

Cowboy allows you bring in eye exchange your companion throughout sex, while the cyclist encounters away in a opposite cowboy.

5. Fisting

Occasionally, utilizing your palms throughout sex could be an excellent method to boost your partner's G-spot or even P-spot without utilizing a penis or even strap-on.

Fisting makes use of your whole palm to pass through your companion through beginning sluggish as well as utilizing bunches of lube to glide in as well as out.

6. Corroded trombone

Occasionally, covering does not need to include infiltration in any way.

To participate in the corroded trombone, your companion kneels on all of fours while you conduct analingus as well as provide a palm project. This sex placement generates a consolidated feeling that can easily sense remarkable for your companion.

Printed in Great Britain
by Amazon